Voices from a Pandemic

poems by

Ellen Hernandez

Finishing Line Press
Georgetown, Kentucky

Voices from a Pandemic

Copyright © 2021 by Ellen Hernandez
ISBN 978-1-64662-490-4 First Edition
All rights reserved under International and Pan-American Copyright Conventions. No part of this book may be reproduced in any manner whatsoever without written permission from the publisher, except in the case of brief quotations embodied in critical articles and reviews.

ACKNOWLEDGMENTS

Thank you to the friends and family who were willing to set aside vulnerability and express their deepest feelings for the well-being of all of us. I feel closer to each of you—Imane, Sanae, Hassan, Kathy, Lydia, Gerry, Debbie, Carrie, Steve, Marc, Chrissie, Jack, Michael, Susie, Wanda, Kelly, Gloria, Solveig, Danna, Terri, Mia, Afra, and Mary Ann. Together, we are sending love and healing out into the world.

Thank you to my colleagues and friends, Matt Sorrento and Pete Woodworth, for their support and insights. I look forward to working with you in person in the after-time.

Finally, thank you to my daughter, Mia, and my husband, Rich, for your love and support and your help with editing the manuscript. I am grateful to have been quarantined with the both of you, and I will always treasure this time.

Publisher: Leah Huete de Maines
Editor: Christen Kincaid
Cover and Interior Art: Afra Stenstrom
Author Photo: Ellen Hernandez
Cover Design: Elizabeth Maines McCleavy

Order online: www.finishinglinepress.com
also available on amazon.com

Author inquiries and mail orders:
Finishing Line Press
PO Box 1626
Georgetown, Kentucky 40324
USA

Table of Contents

Impression (G. Hernandez) 1

Contact (L. Dougherty) 2

Inside (M. A. Ewing Popolizio) 3

Entertaining Self-Control (S. Mead) 4

Isolation (W. Hernandez-Tong) 5

Worrisome (C. Lynn) 6

Absence (M. Kubit) 8

When Everything Stopped (H. Hisse) 9

A Different Normal (K. A. Jackson) 11

Slower Time (M. Hernandez) 13

Hard Lessons for a Better Life (T. Rozzini) 14

A Tough Adjustment (M. Villone) 15

Bored (G. Durisin) 16

Resilience (K. Dawson-Faul) 18

Life Away from the Workplace (J. Pesda) 19

Slowing Down (D. Greenstein) 20

Inventory of a Simpler Life (S. Harris) 21

A Prayer for Normalcy (I. Akhezzane) 22

Trust (S. Ewing Schendel) 23

Clinging to God (C. Hanson) 24

Time for the Earth (S. Benaadim) 25

Healing (D. Davis Daly) 26

Author Notes 28

*To Rich—my rock, my touchstone, the one who
makes it possible for me to dream*

*And to all of the people on the front lines
who are helping, feeding, and healing,
the ones who are sacrificing their safety for the rest of us*

Foreword

Flying home from a visit to my mother in Florida, I was shocked to find an almost-abandoned security area at the airport. On the plane, I was unsettled to see passengers wearing masks and wiping the armrests and food trays. By the time we landed in Philadelphia, I was sufficiently unnerved and knew that what had been a breaking news item about a rapidly-spreading virus had now become an apparent crisis. On the ride home, I could see that streets and parking lots were empty, and on the radio, we heard about shortages at grocery stores. Soon, we learned that we would not be returning to our workplaces. We exchanged urgent messages with friends and family. Thus began a period of ongoing self-quarantine, remote work, and personal protection with my husband and adult daughter that is unlike any I have ever experienced in my life.

The global COVID-19 pandemic has changed the way we live, work, and communicate. In addition to the tragedies of illness and death, unemployment and destitution, it has also interrupted human connection and creativity. We had to find new ways to express ourselves without the traditional venues for theater, musical performance, and authors' readings. Yet, the need to express ourselves artistically has not lessened; if anything, it has grown more pressing as a way to cope.

This collection of poems resulted from a writing project I initiated during the early months of isolation. They were collaboratively written from contributors' reflections in an attempt to record our observations, tend to our mental health during a time of severe stress, and, perhaps, bring some healing to one another.

Those who contributed the works herein were asked to consider and remark on their isolation, their work, their daily lives, and the worldwide situation; to describe how they, their friends, and their families were impacted; and to offer the lessons they were learning. We whose works appear on these pages represent different genders, sexualities, ethnicities and skin colors; different nationalities, ages, marital statuses, educational backgrounds, and languages; different work situations, domiciles, political views, and religions. The pandemic is our common experience, and our need to make sense of this moment in history and survive it—together—is our common goal.

We offer these as a gift in the hope that the reader can find solace.

—Ellen Hernandez

Impression
Gloria Hernandez

We take
life
for granted

Contact
Lydia Dougherty

It is honestly creepy,
way too quiet,
stressful.

I am not working,
waiting for a call-back,
or network access
to actually work
from home.

I feel conscious,
spiritual,
hopeful.

I almost enjoy the unsettling quiet.

I cannot *wait* to get back
to seeing my friends
on the bus.

More aware of the need to see friends,
no more "I don't have time,"
traveling as soon as I can.

We are in better contact now:
hearing people
and myself
apologizing
for not taking time
to be in touch.

We need contact,
physical contact,
to survive.

Inside
Mary Ann Ewing Popolizio

Staying inside,
just making mailbox trips,
I feel lucky
to have a back patio
overlooking a lake.

I am frightened
and feel helpless.

Retired,
I communicate
by phone or computer
and spend too much time
on the couch.

I see nothing positive,
just anxiety and worry
over faraway family.

I wonder how long
before normalcy returns
to the planet.

Entertaining Self-Control
Solveig Mead

I only go outside
for short walks.

It's scary,
this mostly-inside staying,
this not-very-uplifting time.

Retired,
I miss volunteering
but am glad for
concerned neighbors
and more cars at home,

Keeping in touch
by phone and Face Time,
people are taking this virus
more seriously.

Isolation
Wanda Hernandez-Tong

Isolated,
in a remote part of Guyana,
stepping outside my door
I am in the Amazon jungle.

Yearning for my children
in Miami,
I could leave,
could contact the embassy,
but am safer here
though people are uneducated,
un-masked,
un-distanced,

Food is a 40-minute drive,
so, we garden.
We grow our own,
depend on no one,
learn to be self-sufficient.

It's rough on us all.

Worrisome
Christine Lynn

Worried,
only leaving home for necessities,
I see others like me
and am shocked,
questioning my own reasons.

Caution translates to
a pharmacy drive-through,
a bank teller's drawer,
rubber gloves,
a sanitized pen,
a construction mask,
Lysol wipes,
the horror of a cashier's cough into her gloved fist.

How often do I touch my face?

Undistracted by homeschooled children,
I can focus on work
Uninterrupted,
gratefully free from an hour-long commute,
another pointless meeting,
a micromanaging supervisor.
This work life is freeing,
productive,
peaceful.

My happiness is tainted
by uncertainty,
the frightening human hoarding habit,
the dreadful waiting.

I worry about a friend with cancer,
a sister's surgery,
my mother's compromised condition,
a brother-in-law's lost job,
and I am learning
nothing is more important
than family,
friends,
kindness,
good health.

Absence
Marc Kubit

It is very quiet,
this absence of noisy planes,
this distance-keeping,
and it makes us anxious.

Work has not changed,
just my boundary limits.
I miss the face-to-face,
and I worry
about family's and friends' health.

I feel frustrated,
anxious,
and angry,
but the long-wished-for absence
of D.C.'s "cancerous growth"
gets closer.

Elected officials need competency tests
and background transparency
in advance.

When Everything Stopped
Hassan Hisse

I am not allowed in the streets.
The police are everywhere—
it's crazy.

There is no work for me now—
All my work has stopped

It's hard for me to focus my thoughts,
confusing and unbelievable.

The streets are empty—
Banks stop at 2pm,
Grocery stops at 6pm,
Quiet,
like a ghost city.

There is fresh air,
less traffic,
fewer accidents.
We really can breathe again
but the silence is very scary.

I still hear the call to prayer—
very clear,
clearer.
It gives me comfort,
gives everyone comfort.

I am alone in my flat.
I like it.
It is good for me,
for others.

I am good.
My parents are good,
my brother,
my family,
all good.

They don't work.
No one works now.

A Different Normal
Kelly A. Jackson

I go out every few days
for groceries
or take out.

Markedly fewer cars—
small clusters in
strip mall parking lots—
places are open.

You might not know
anything is wrong.

Isolated,
concerned,
angry—
it's unpredictable.

Moving from
someone in my state to
someone in my county to
someone I know to
someone I love,
commitment to distancing changes.

Exponential growth
un-comprehended—
even a little bit—
people grow angry at
economic impact and
personal liberties lost.

For my in-laws,
business may go under
where there aren't even cases.
Abiding by the order,
social distancing is
literally
causing bankruptcy.

"All politics is local"—
"global" is too big
to consider,
too big to fathom.

I've taken the "me" out of
my teaching.
Power points,
annotated notes,
pre-recorded lectures—
nice, but not
what makes "my class"
mine.

Yes, future classes will be better
from my lessons learned.

My family unit found
a different normal,
not all bad.

I miss my dad.

Slower Time
    Mia Hernandez

Three of us
in a two-story house
still need more space
on top of each other,
stressed and tired
of the same faces,
lonely
in our togetherness.

No place to go
even if I go out.

My headset on,
I call empty offices
and ghost-worker voice mail.

Yet,

It's a quieter, slower world
with cleaner air.

Things don't have to
go back to
"normal"
to be better.

Hard Lessons for a Better Life
Terri Rozzini

Sadly,
I only travel outside
for groceries, or
medical appointments
with my husband.

Hard lessons learned
from financial blow,
lost jobs,
lost investments,
teach me
America
needs a return
to independence.

Daily life is healthier,
enlightening,
peaceful.

Good food,
prepared, presented properly,
pizza-making skills perfected,
restaurant food no longer appeals.

Air pollution,
no longer obscures
the western mountains.

A Tough Adjustment
Michael Villone

My husband's arrival home
entails clothing decontamination—
stripped down and straight into the wash—
his work now a tough adjustment for us both.

Seeing people wearing gloves
and face masks (incorrectly)
scares me.

Quite hard, this inability
to see in-laws and grandparents,
nieces and nephews,
and I am left feeling alone.

The bright spot in the darkness
is humanity seeming to unite.

We are learning to live life frugally,
humbly,
and to take care of ourselves.

Bored
Gerry Durisin

I have not been farther than my own yard
in over two weeks.
It's a bit claustrophobic,
this adjusting,
this finding of ways to keep occupied
in and around the house.
Rainy days are hardest.

Retired, there is no work to change,
but other activities are missed:
local college classes,
theater and concerts,
friend-gatherings,
restaurant outings.

Bored, yet resigned,
and grateful,
for family,
for a comfortable home,
for shelter.

Interludes of solitude
are necessary,
for too much togetherness.

The tv news is painful,
grateful that a daughter's family
escaped from New York
before the bad,
sheltering-in-place with us,
sad another cannot be.

Granddaughters are a wonderful distraction.

Everyone is bored and restless and anxious.

We stay in touch,
by social media,
by phone,
by text.

We can survive anything.

Resilience
Kathy Dawson-Faul

We can go outside,
grateful for two acres of woods
for a husband who needs it,
glad to have room
for waiting this out.

Happy to be retired,
I am upset for loved ones
considered "necessary" workers,
sad and frightened
for their risk.

Lonely and frustrated,
but grateful,
hopeful,
I am determined to appreciate
loved ones and life
even more when this is over.

The human response
is so much selflessness
and positivity.
It makes me grateful
and proud.

Life goes on,
wishing for family-sharing,
still happy that life goes on.
It should.

Life is short.
At best.
People are resilient.

With resilience,
we await our kids
and grandkids
again.

Life away from the Workplace
    Jack Pesda

Long, daily walks
in Ocean City, New Jersey—
America's Greatest Family Resort—
are quite different
when the beaches and boardwalk are closed.
So quiet are the empty streets,
the somber faces,
the silenced voices.

Work has changed
dramatically,
reduced to remote communication,
and I discover
life away from the workplace.

Good marriages blossom
and happy families grow closer,
spending time together, enjoying life's little gifts—
planning a meal,
watching a film,
parents and children visiting
from a distance
while we talk from the porch.

We would love to hug our grandchildren.

Slowing Down
Debbie Greenstein

Surreal,
this staying in,
this only-occasional going-out,
so many out walking,
exercising,
the irony that a virus
might get us in shape.

Happily-retired,
introverted,
I am surprisingly at ease,
my penchant for distancing
no longer seeming weird.

How little I miss
eating out,
being among the cranky,
the wrecked,
the crazy public,
the ones who do not get flu shots,
who do not wonder at those annual deaths.

No one I know is sick.

Most complain about loneliness,
boredom,
but hold up well.

We can afford
to slow down
our hectic pace.

Inventory of a Simpler Life
Steve Harris

Inconceivable,
this restriction to home,
this risky world,
people on edge,
worried about closeness,
keeping disinfected,
our interactions all upended.

My normal job on hold,
travel ceased,
customers transitioning
to this new remote work,
productivity is hampered
by working blind—
it's grim.

Proud of my family—
daughter becoming a distant learner,
wife an online art teacher—
I am grateful
for how life has slowed down,
how time together has a finer quality,
discovering ourselves,
missing our freedoms,
reflecting on what matters
in the inventory of a simpler life.

Most are unified,
working to overcome our situation—
the world entire
experiencing this event together,
the compassionate more compassionate,
neighbor helping neighbor.

We must stop looking
in the rear-view mirror,
focus on the road ahead.

We are all healing
in ways not yet realized.

A Prayer for Normalcy
Imane Akhezzane

Our field work regrettably postponed
and workshops only online,
we work from home.
What I used to do
and now cannot
has greater value.

I watch my parents
here at home,
see their fears,
and family
and time
have greater importance.

Patiently I wait,
sometimes bored,
sometimes scared,
but always hopeful.

Life is very short,
and every moment
makes me grateful,
looking forward to a time
without stress,
without sadness,
with joy,
with normalcy.

Trust
Susie Ewing Schendel

I have not gone out—
there's nowhere to go
but a fast-food drive-through
or a cigarette-run for mom.
It's nothing new, really.

I send my husband out
like Noah sent the birds
to test the waters.

Retired
disabled,
I order online,
intrigued by others' panicking,
their hoarding,
their fear.

I feel connection
with all of humanity
like never before,
a closeness
to heaven's nearness.

Come, Lord Jesus, Come!
Trust in the Lord
with all your heart
and lean not
on your own understanding.

Clinging to God
Carrie Anne Hanson

We go out for walks
around the lake,
get groceries every two weeks
with a mask.

I disinfect everything I touch.

This is challenging,
trying to save our businesses,
just being furloughed,
applying for unemployment
approaching Good Friday,
trusting in God.

How different we all are,
happy pets,
families spending time together,
husbands and wives,
mothers and fathers,
clinging to faith
or finding it,
so different than
half a century ago.

Family and friends—
an ICU nurse,
two police officers—
put in danger
to care for others,
unprotected,
unsupplied.

We can only appreciate what we have,
the basic necessities,
and cling to God
more than ever.

Time for the Earth
Sanae Benaadim

Isolation,
at home,
keeps me safe—
a blessing.

My team collaborates,
coordinates,
communicates,
tries to make progress.

Family and friends become more important,
our relationships stronger,
staying positive,
optimistic,
as much as we can.

Now is the time
for Earth to update itself—
get clean of pollution—
for us to think about life,
appreciate the little things
we used to have,
and get closer to God.

Healing
Danna Davis-Daly

We are allowed out
for shopping,
to get medicines or see a doctor,
for once-a-day exercise, two kilometers.
I am avoiding the shops.

Daily, the children and I walk with the dogs.
I absolutely enjoy this time
Immensely.
Streets are quiet,
enlightening.

Essentially unemployed,
receiving a much-appreciated benefit,
I do short online videos
for my music students,
engaging during homeschooling.

Days are cyclical,
karmic,
challenging.
There is a karmic healing inside.

People around the globe
experiencing isolation,
its challenges,
my feelings of physical and emotional isolation
validated.
I feel connected.

Noticing a gratitude,
feelings of busyness suppressed
coming to the surface,
and often a need to rest.
Huge anger/grief being healed.

More relaxed with my children,
fewer arguments,
very used to house isolation
from the before-time of
years of illness
makes an easier transition.

No phone chats with friends—
short texts,
social media.

Quite emotionally tired
from the process
of isolation,
feeling a progress.

Death is part of life:
cannot escape it,
the fear or denial of it
motivates
every action we take
while alive.

Either in trying to make the best of every moment
in hopes of being remembered after death
or in trying to control our fear of death,
human behavior, in this respect,
varies very little across land borders.

Author Notes

Imane Akhezzane (A Prayer for Normalcy) is a marketing manager and project manager at a Moroccan-U.S. non-governmental organization. She is from Morocco.

Sanae Benaadim (Time for the Earth) is working at the High Atlas Foundation as an office manager and volunteer coordinator. She is a Moroccan citizen.

Danna Davis-Daly (Healing) is a professional singer, actress, voice-over specialist, and musical theater performance coach living in Ireland but originally from New York.

Kathy Dawson-Faul (Resilience) is a retired educator from New Jersey.

Lydia Dougherty (Contact) is a mother of five from Pittsburgh, Pennsylvania.

Susie Ewing Schendel (Trust) is a retired social worker and training developer from Oak Ridge, Tennessee.

Gerry Durisin (Bored) is a retired special educator who currently resides in New Jersey.

Debbie Greenstein (Slowing Down) is a retired but still-passionate public educator.

Carrie Anne Hanson (Clinging to God) is an animal rights activist from New York.

Steven Harris (Inventory of a Simpler Life) is an executive and educator within the telecommunication industry, from New Jersey.

Gloria Hernandez (Impression) is a retired mother of three from Brooklyn, New York.

Mia Hernandez (Slower Time) is a student in Pennsylvania.

Wanda Hernandez-Tong (Isolation) is a nurse from Miami, Florida.

Hassan Hisse (When Everything Stopped) is a tour leader in Morocco.

Kelly A. Jackson (A Different Normal) is a math professor at Camden County College.

Marc Kubit (Absence) is retired after 40 years from being a high school guidance counselor at Tilden High School in Brooklyn and Herricks High School, Long Island, NY.

Christine Lynn (Worrisome) is an English professor in New Jersey.

Solveig Mead (Entertaining Self-Control) is a retired Pan Am flight attendant from Norway living in southern Florida.

John Pesda (Life Away from the Workplace) is a history professor in New Jersey.

Mary Ann Ewing Popolizio (Inside) is a retired secretary and a proud grandmother living in Florida.

Terri Rozzini (Hard Lessons for a Better Life) is a horse trainer living in Arizona.

Afra Stenstrom (photos) is a photographer living in California, originally from Mexico.

Michael Villone (A Tough Adjustment) is just your average, everyday citizen, loving husband, and father to four cats.

Ellen Hernandez is a writer and educator living in southern New Jersey, USA. She holds a B.A. in English literature and language and a Master's in education and English literature. She is the co-author of the textbook *Portfolios: A Guide for Writing Students* (McGraw-Hill) and author of the textbook *Writing for All* (2nd edition, Cognella, Inc., 2019) as well as a chapter in *Exploring Downton Abbey: Critical Essays* (Scott Stoddard, ed., McFarland & Co., 2018). Her previous poetry collection, *In Morocco: rihlat aimra'at 'amrikia*, was published in 2019 (Finishing Line Press). She is studying the Arabic language in the hopes of returning to North Africa to work toward peace between people.

-All authors' proceeds will be donated to charity-

www.ingramcontent.com/pod-product-compliance
Lightning Source LLC
LaVergne TN
LVHW041505070426
835507LV00012B/1328